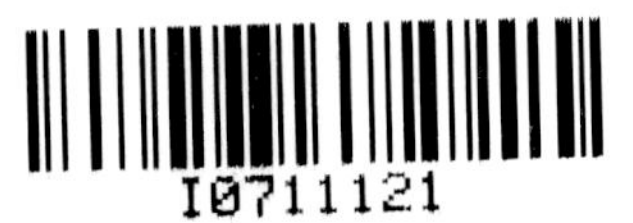

UNCLE SAM'S OFFFICIAL USA 2020 ELECTION COLORING BOOK

A Therapeutic Coloring Experience

Reynold Greenleaf

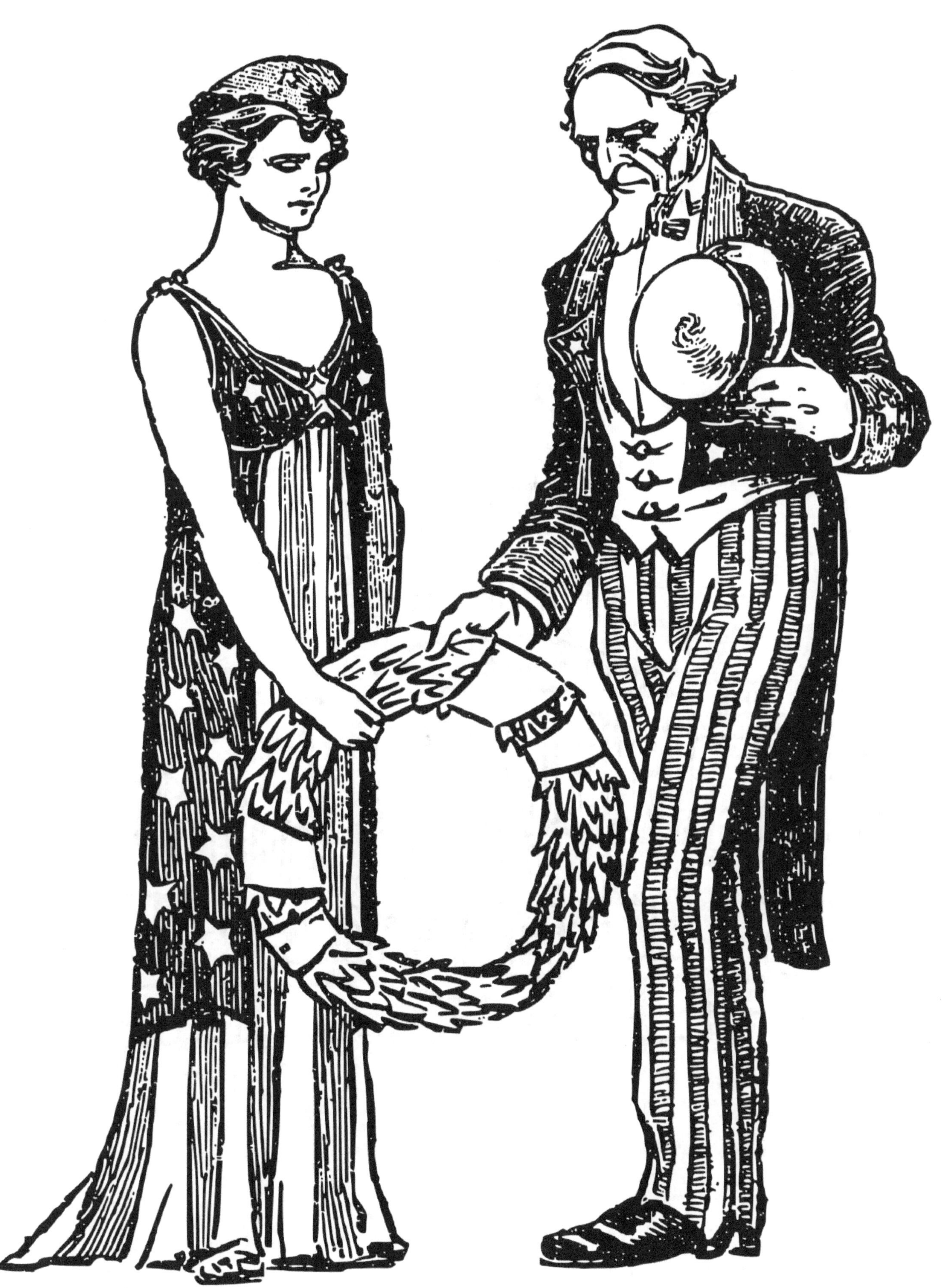

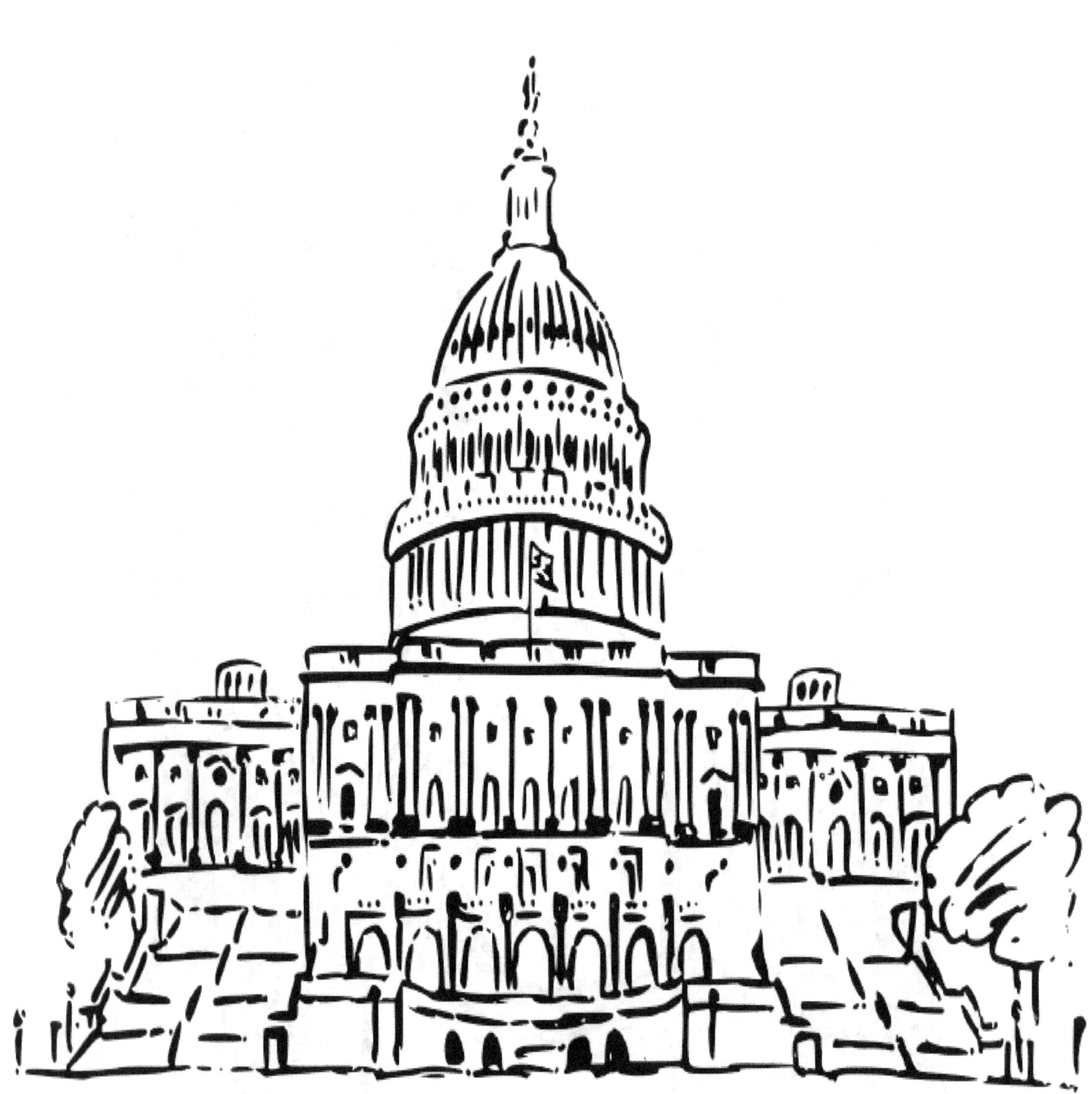

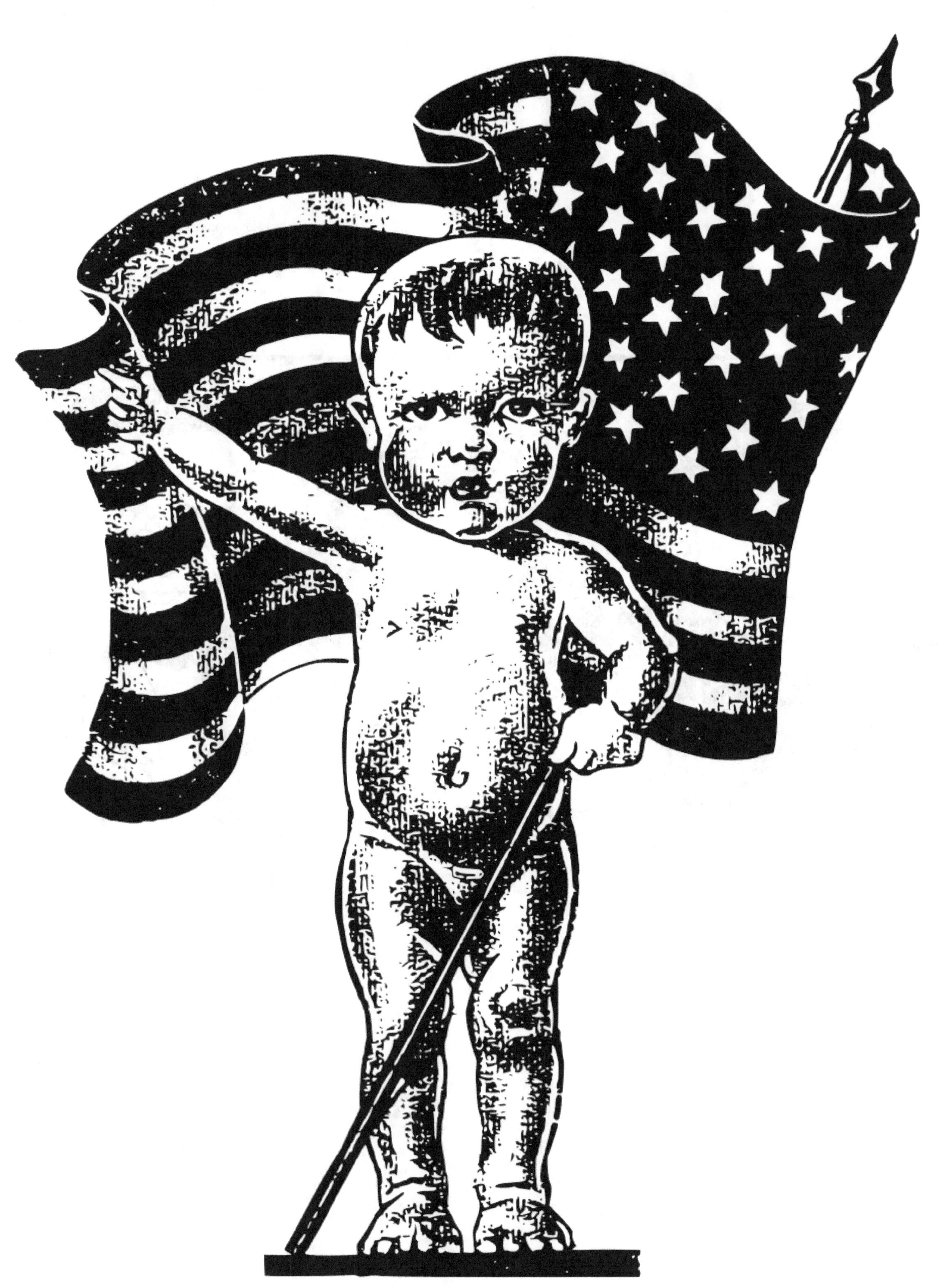

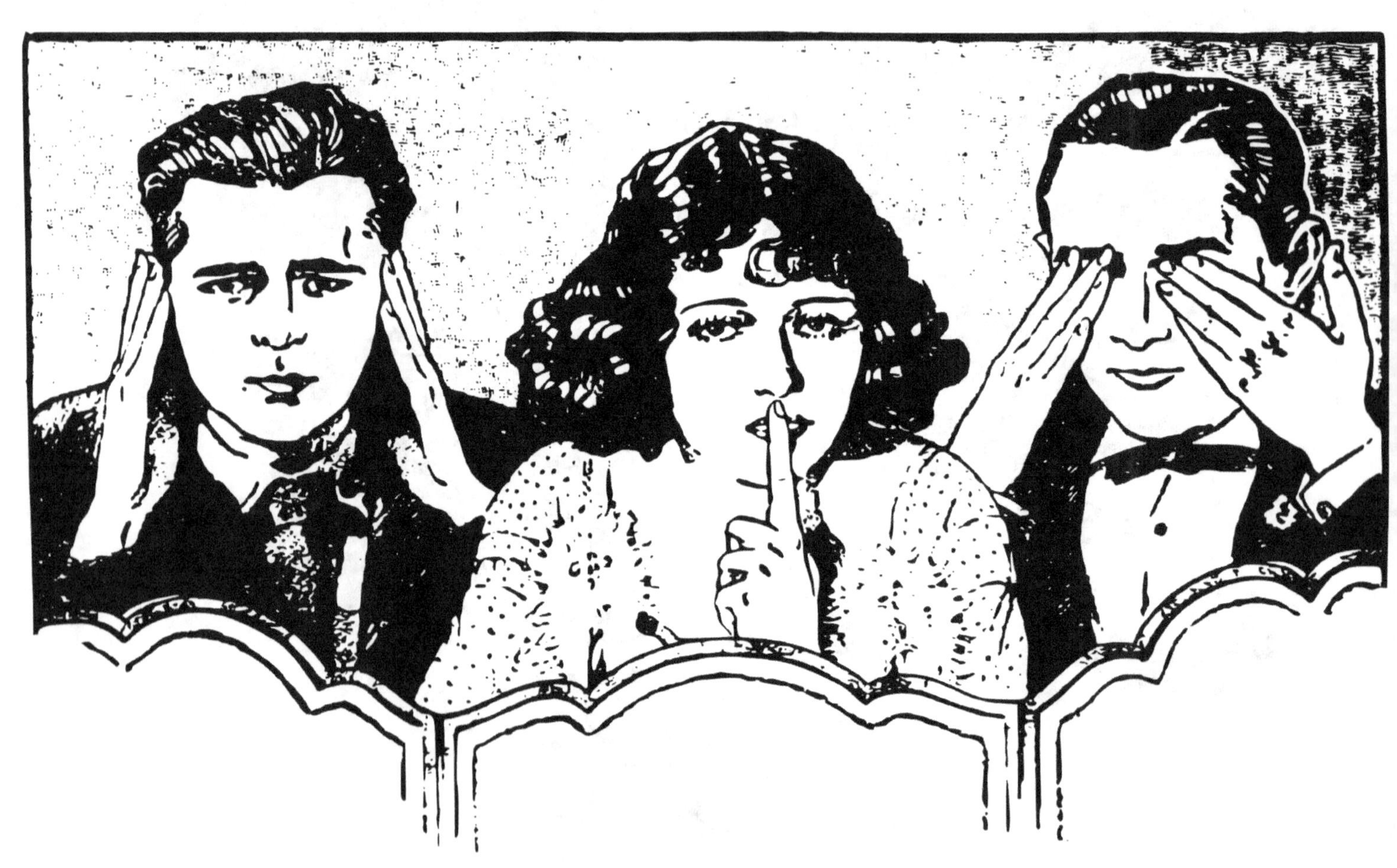

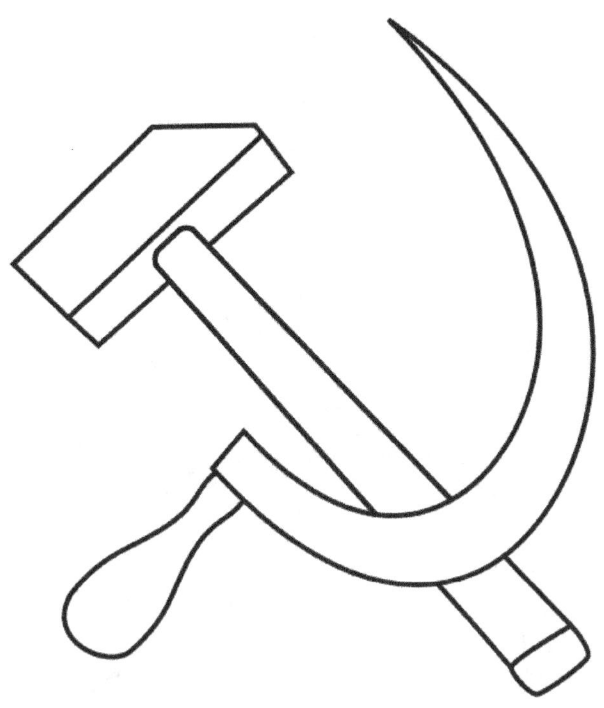

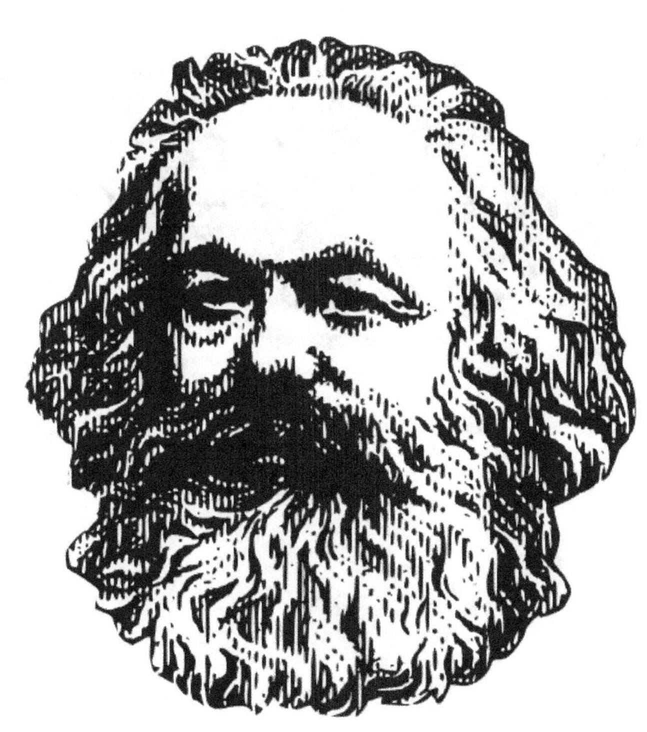

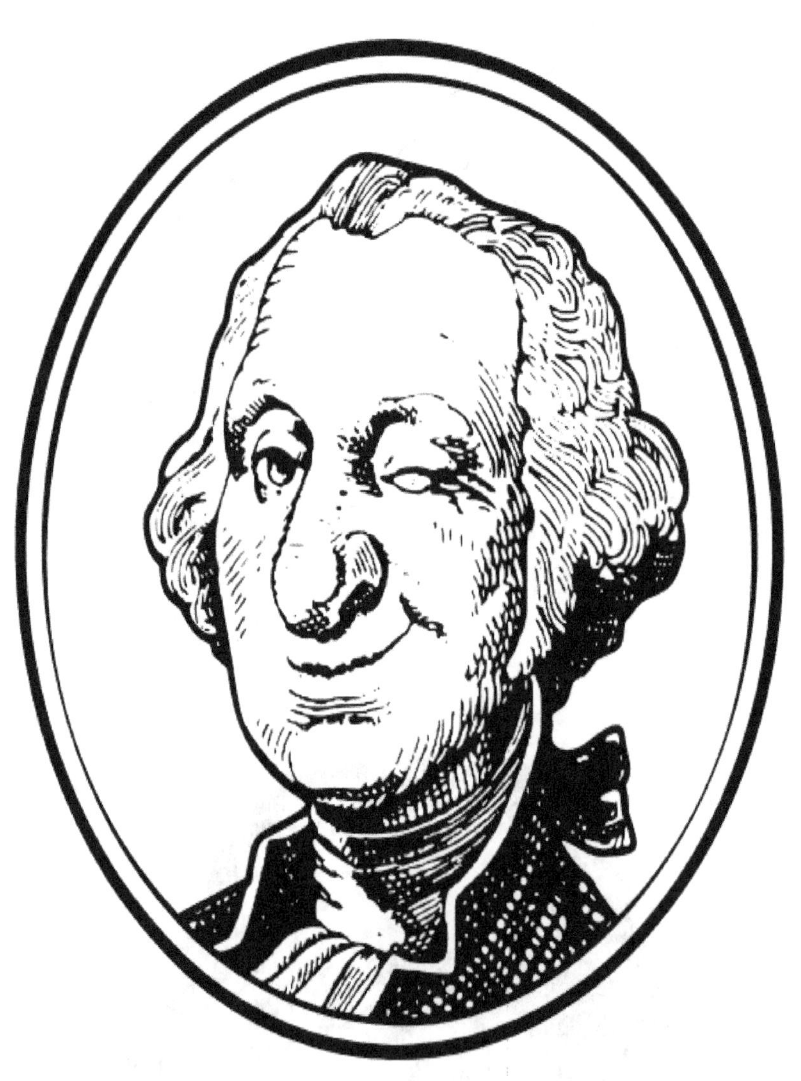

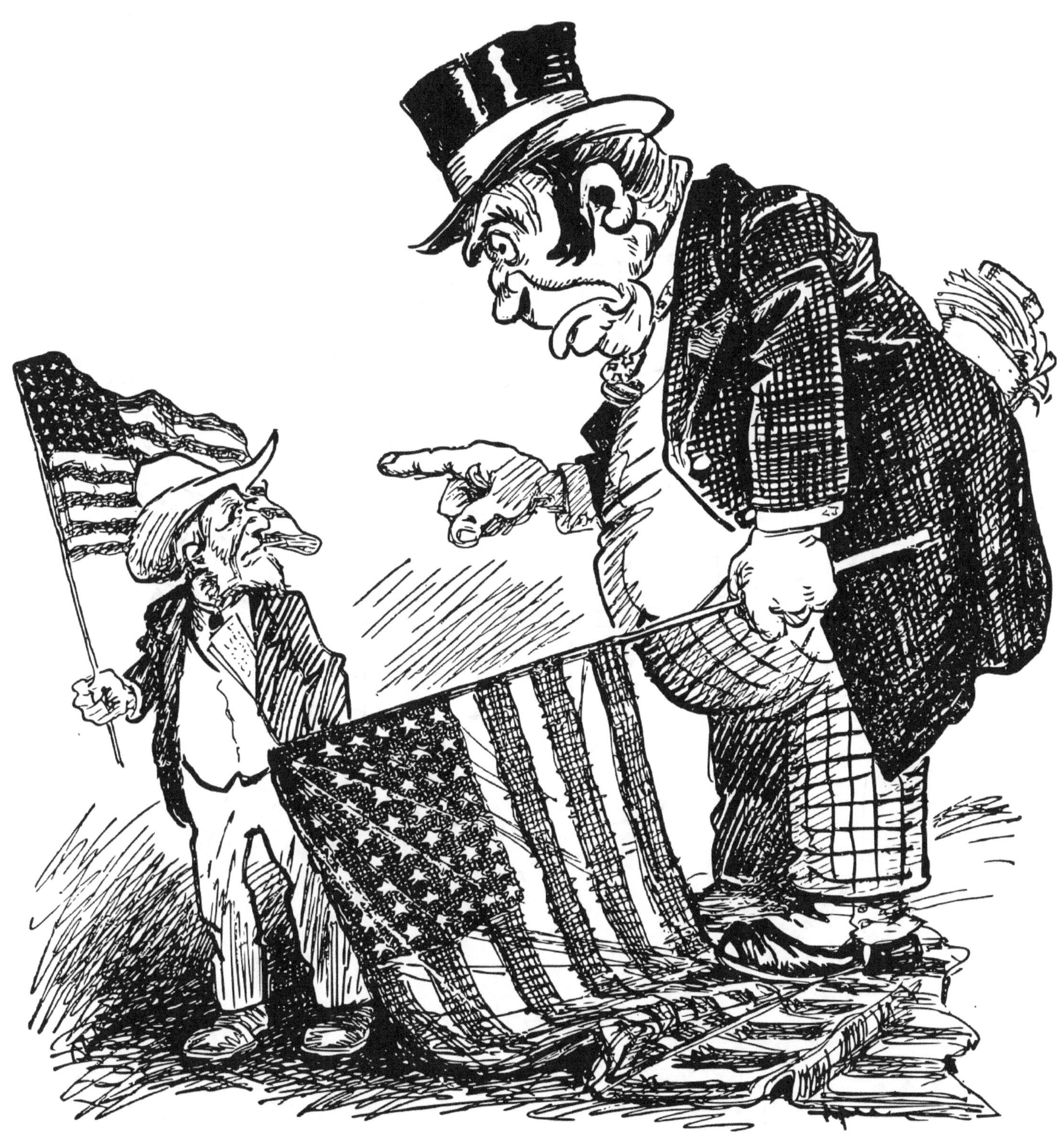

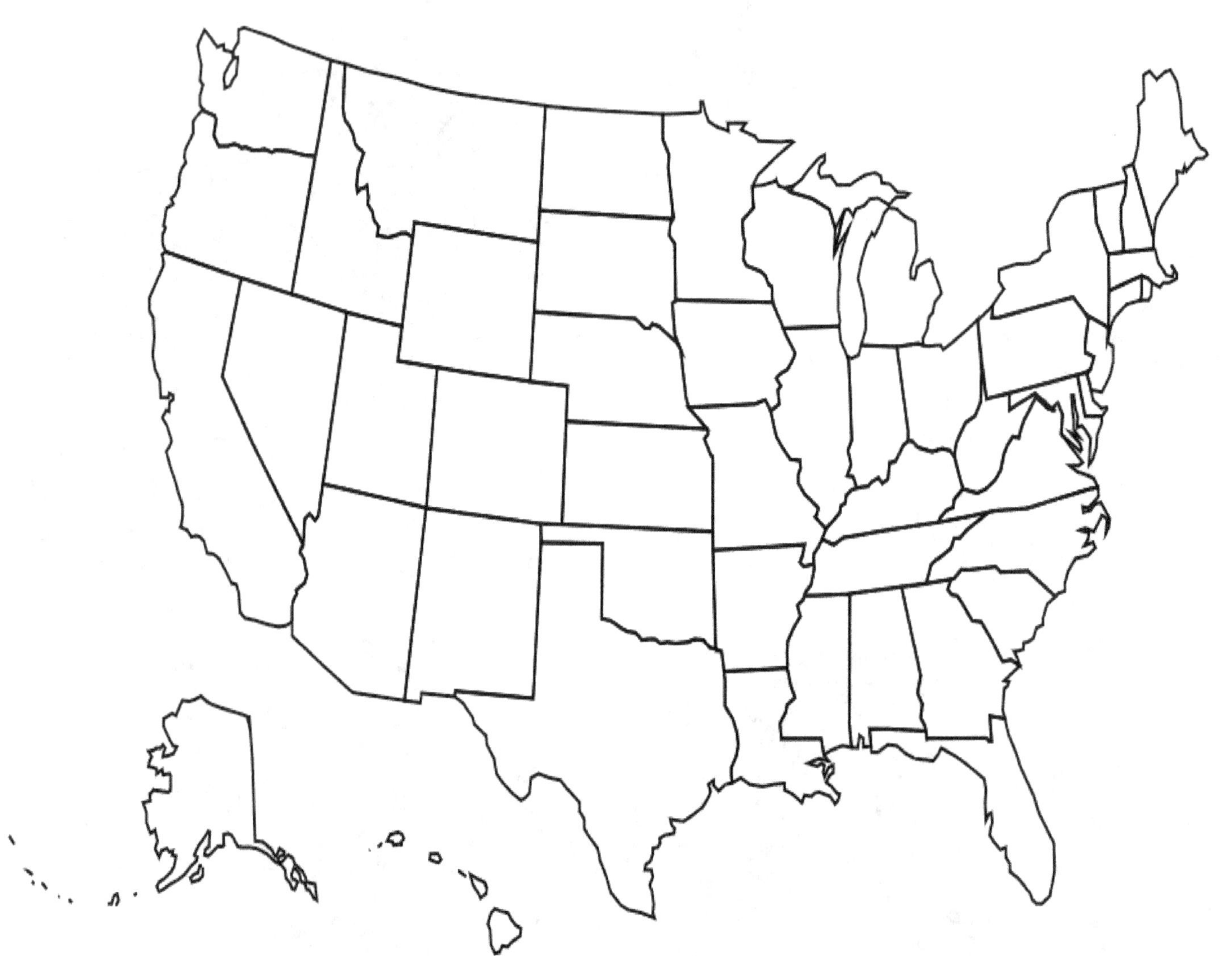

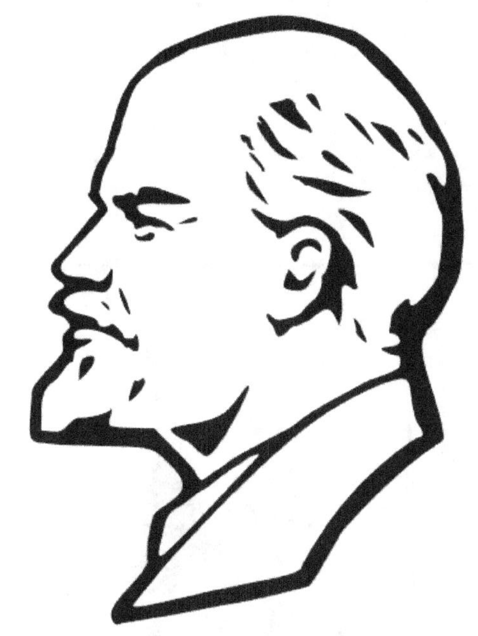

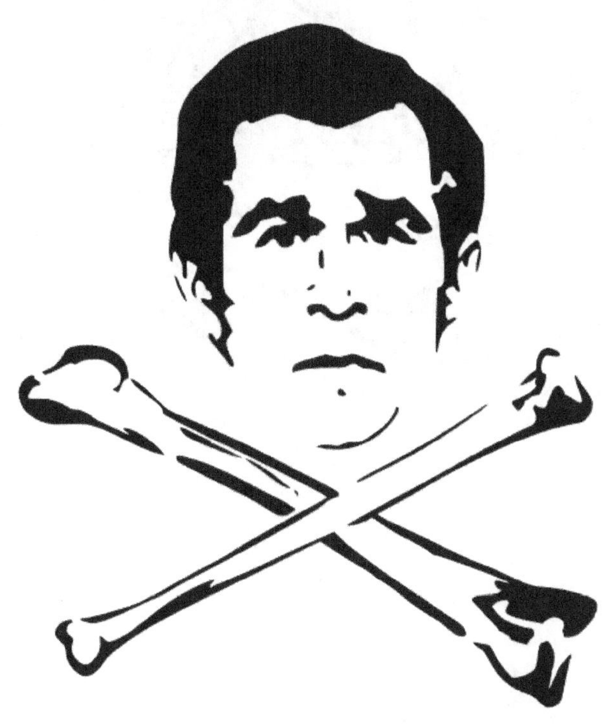

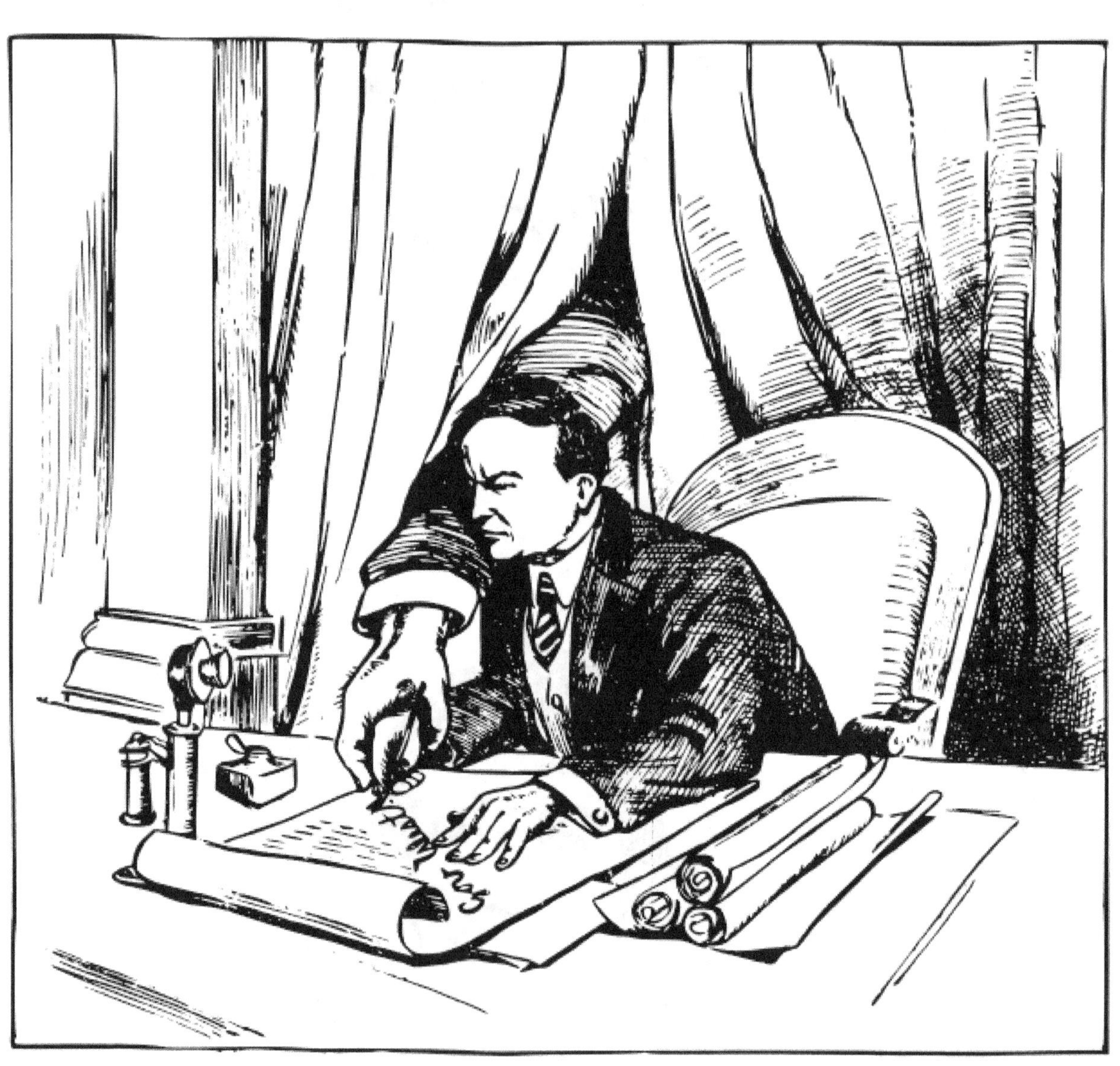

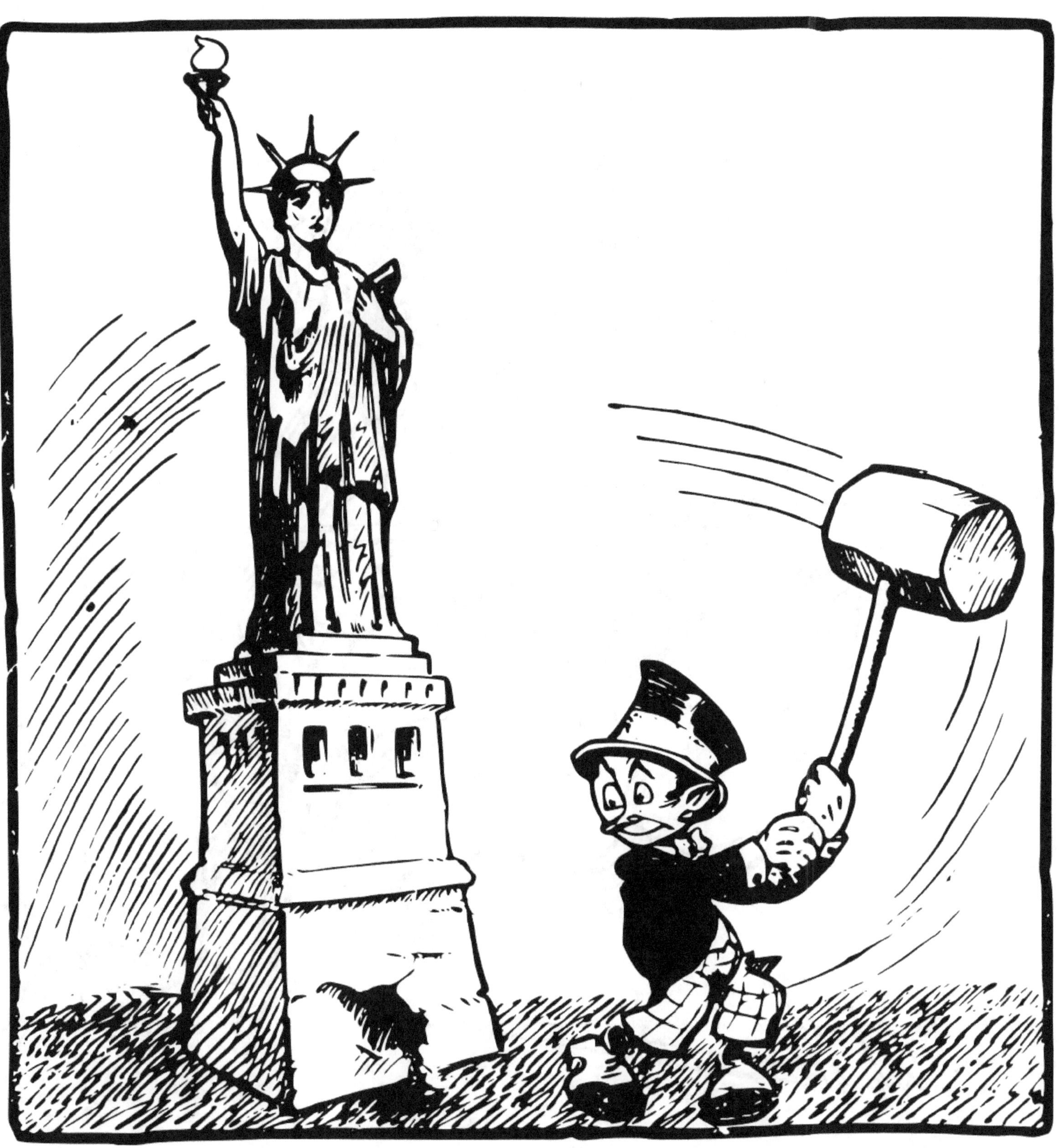

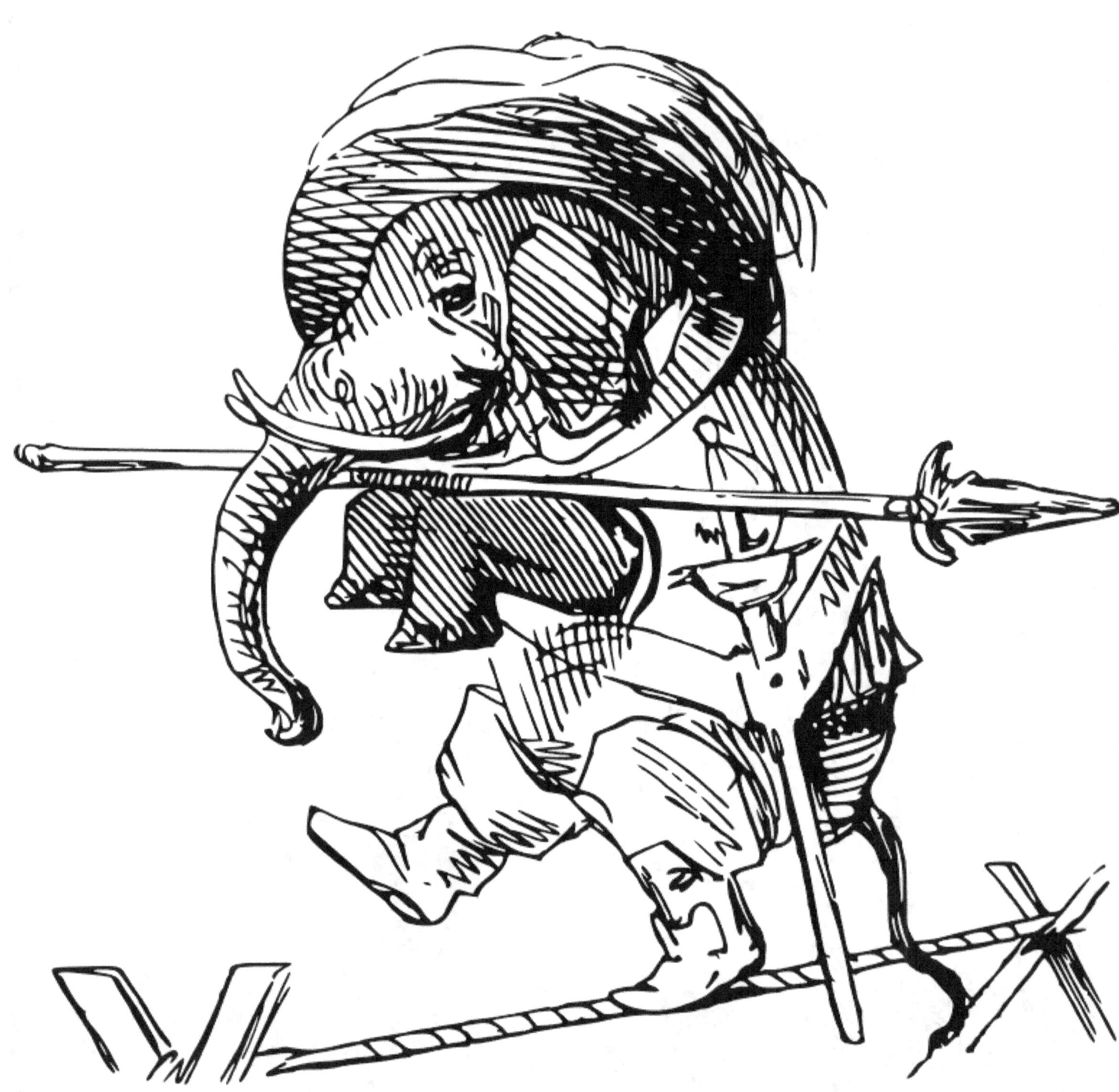

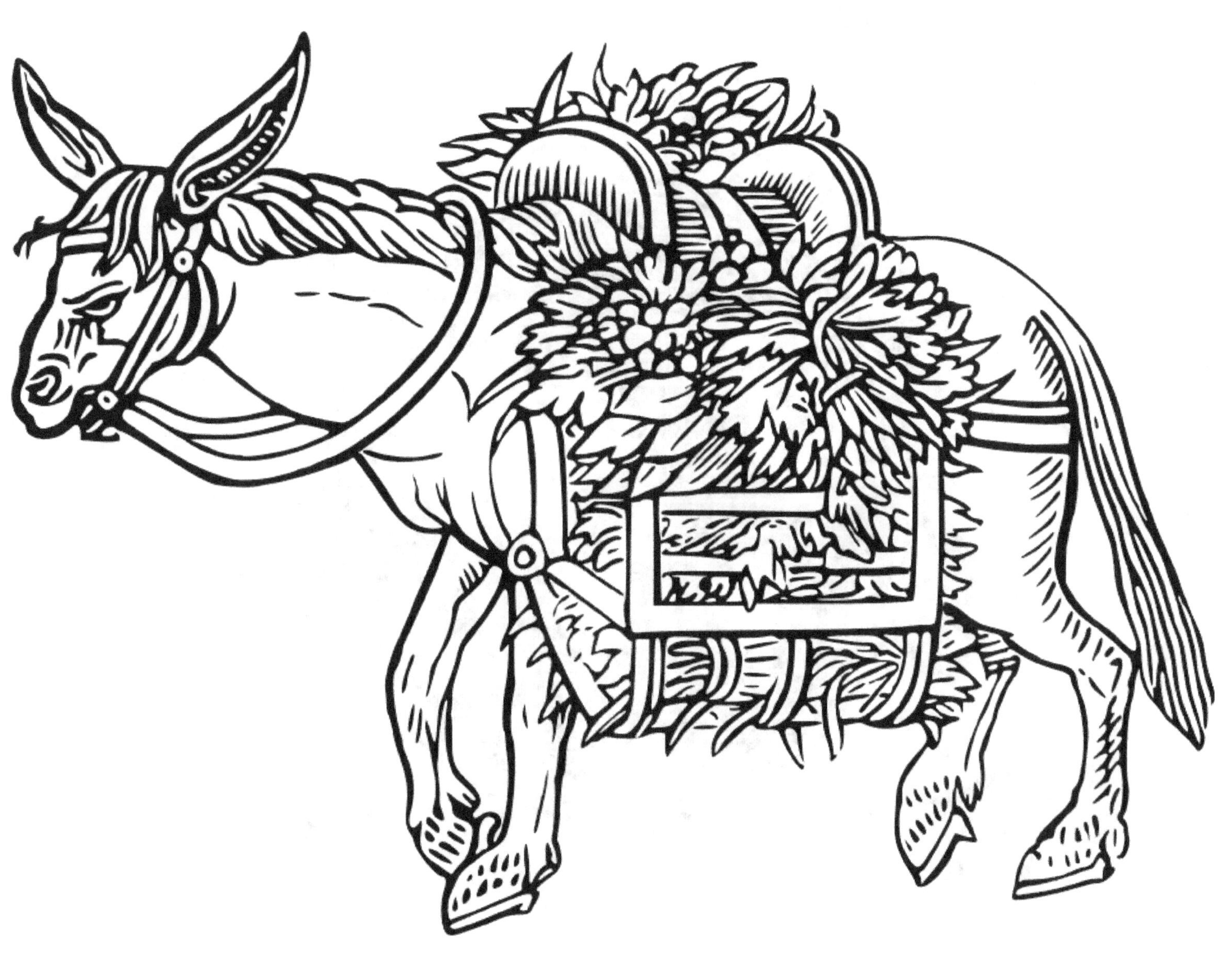

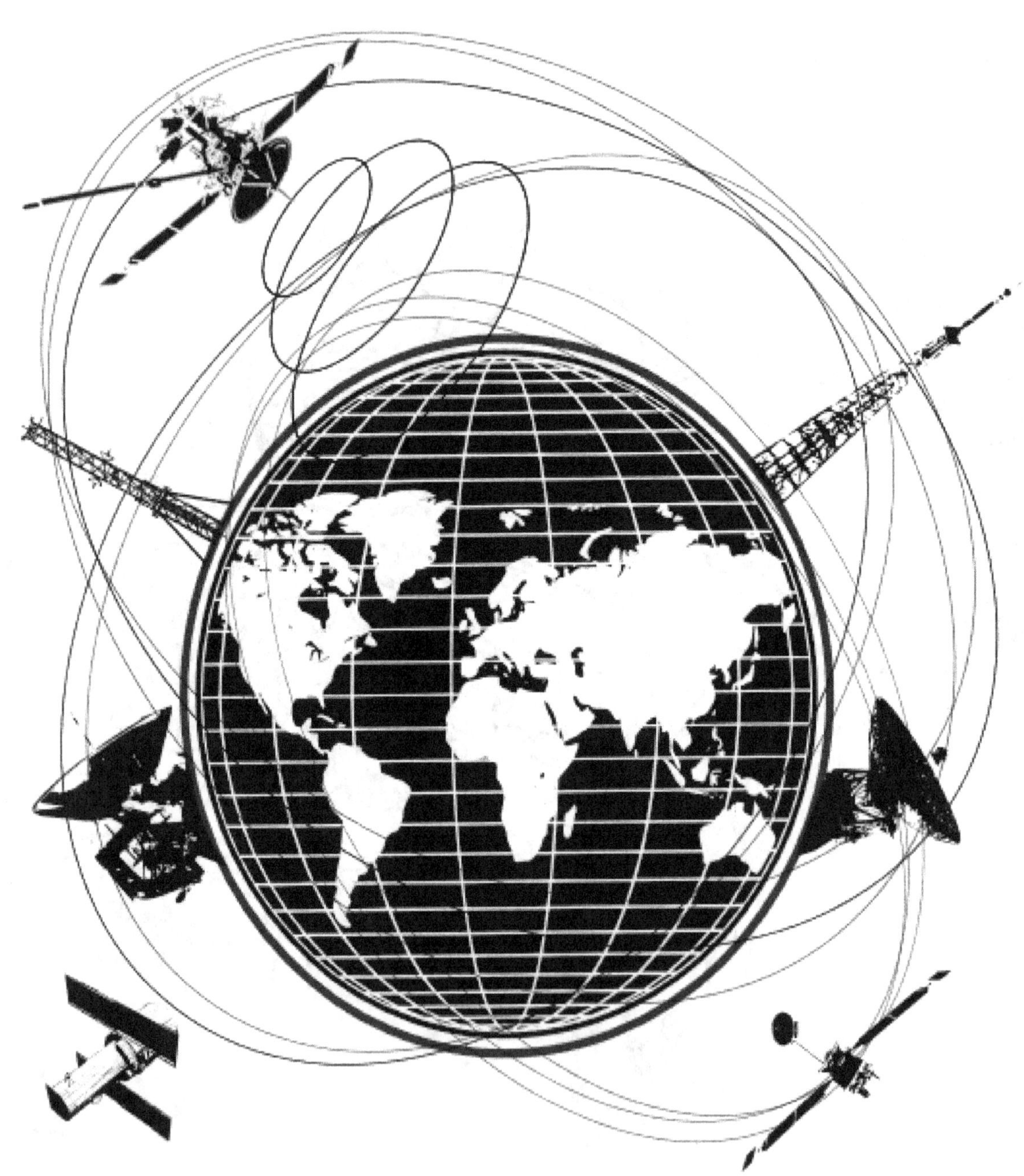

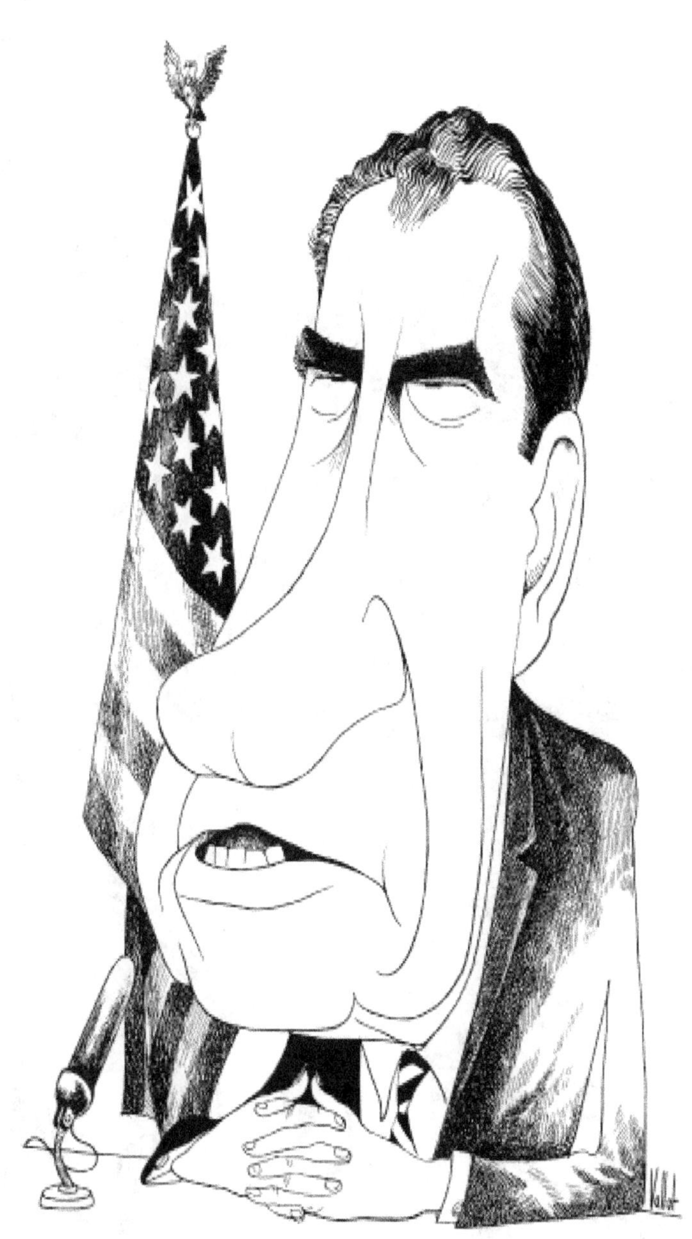

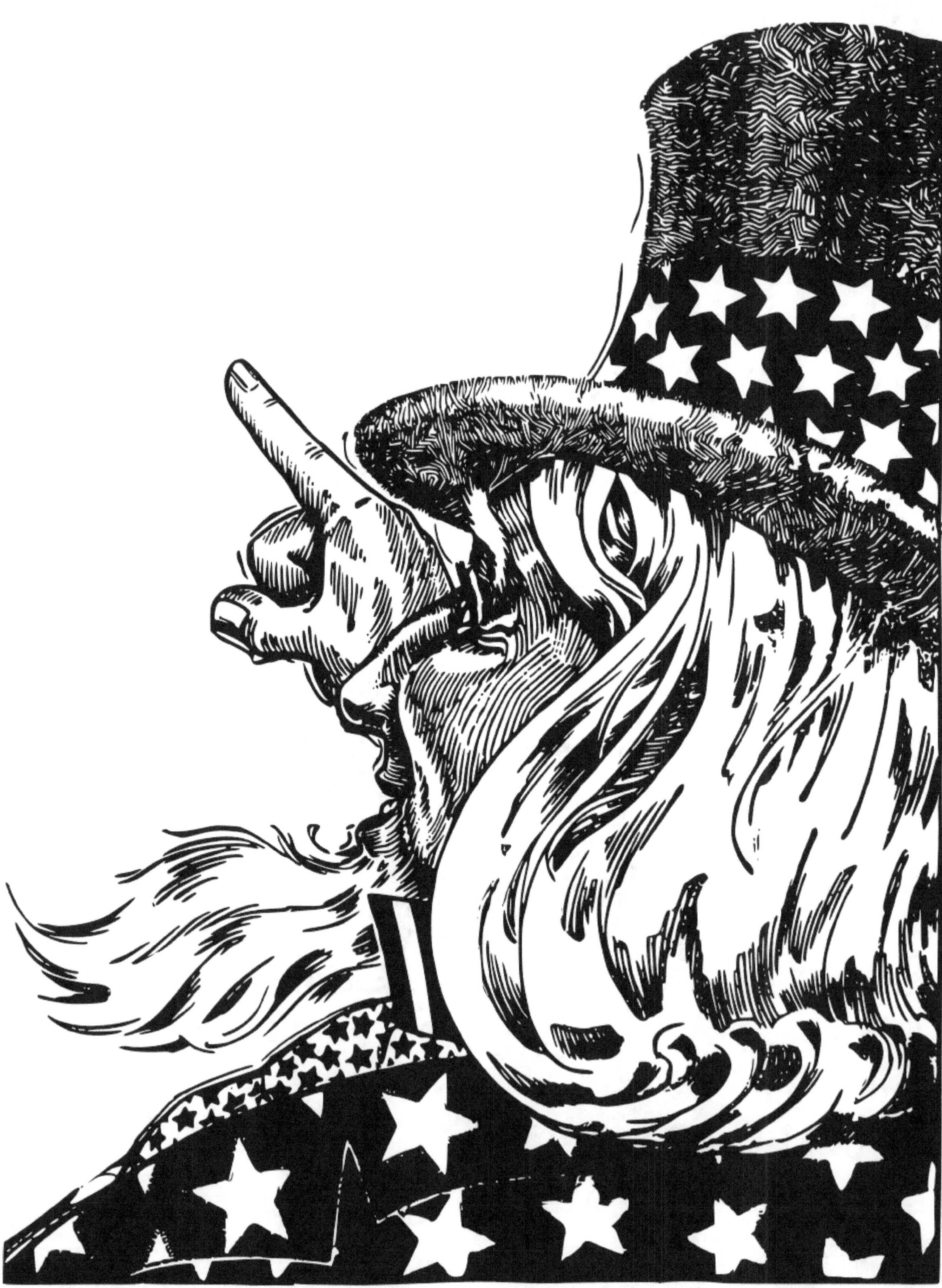

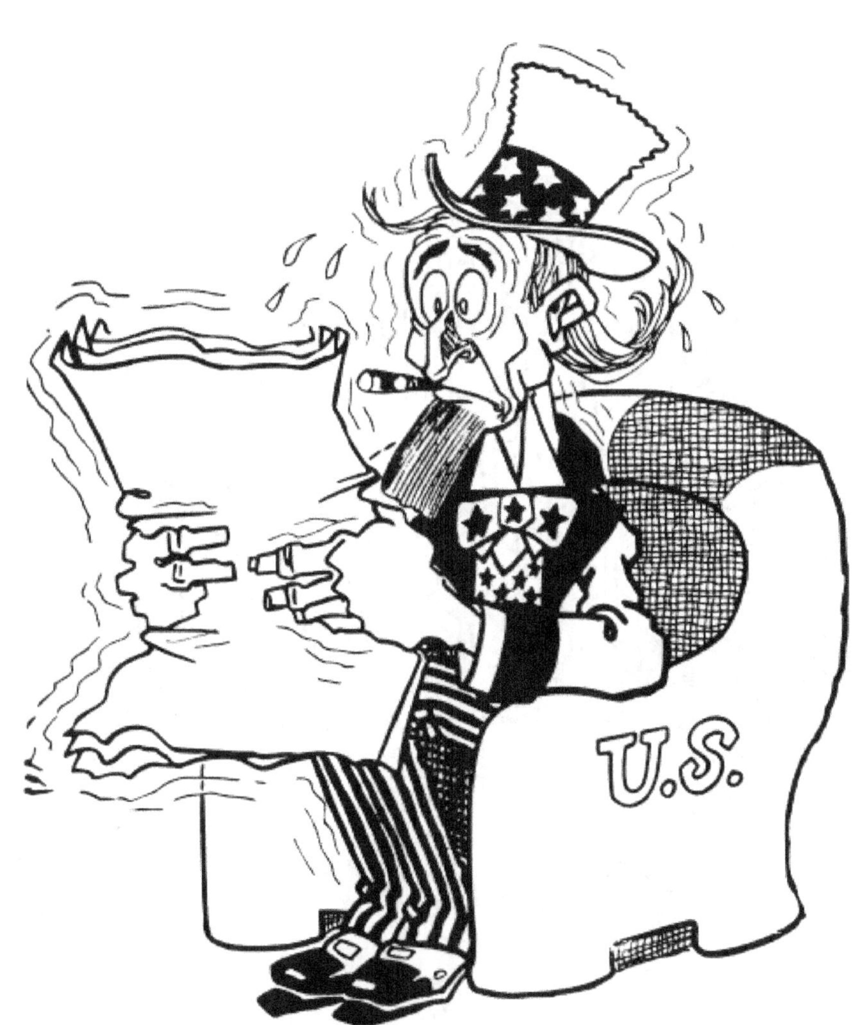
U.S.

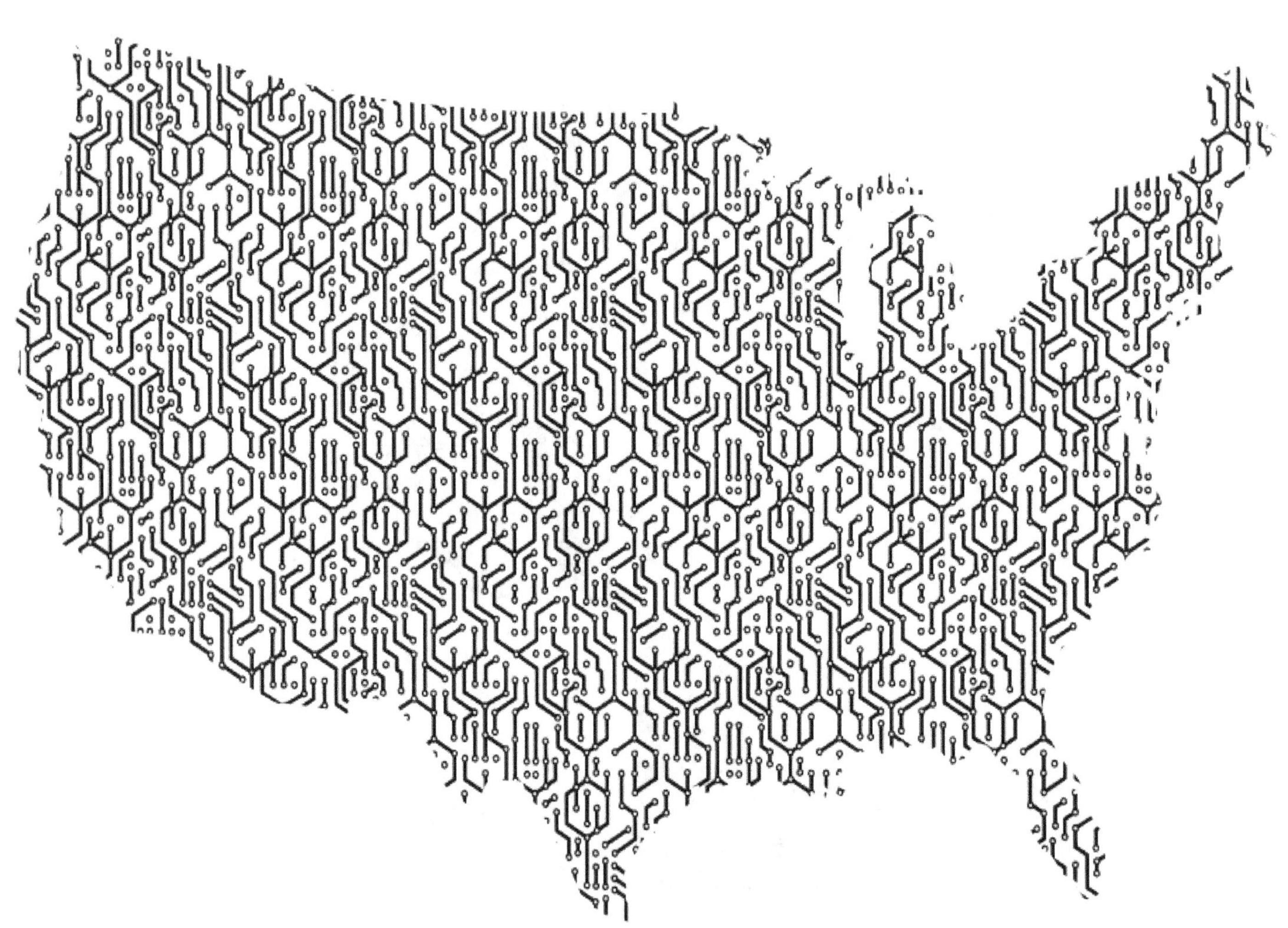

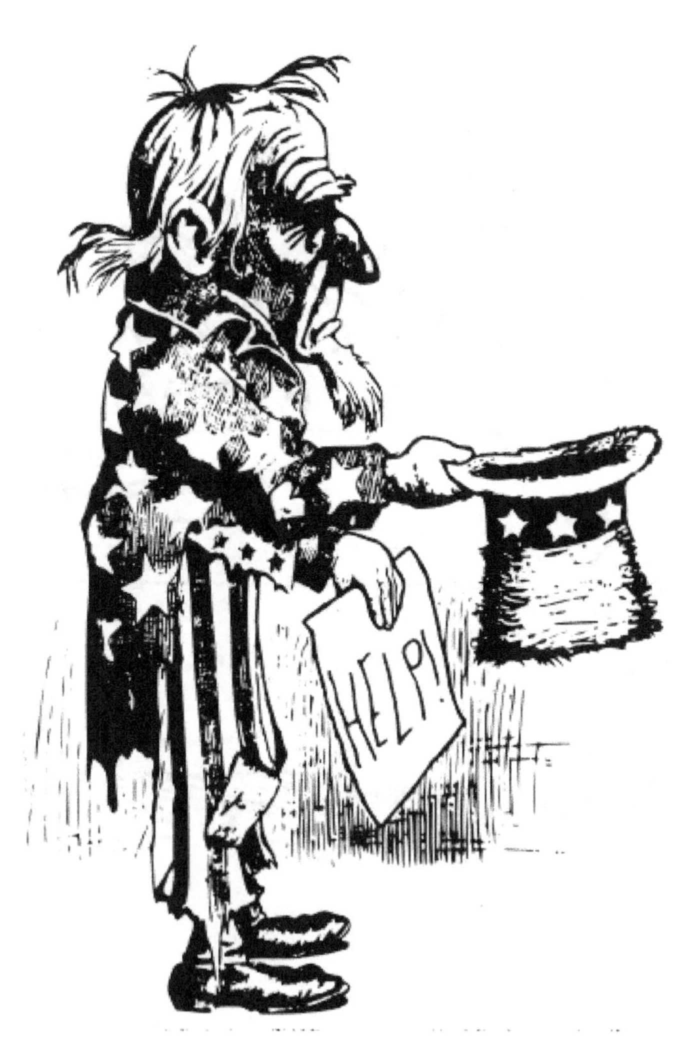

HELP!

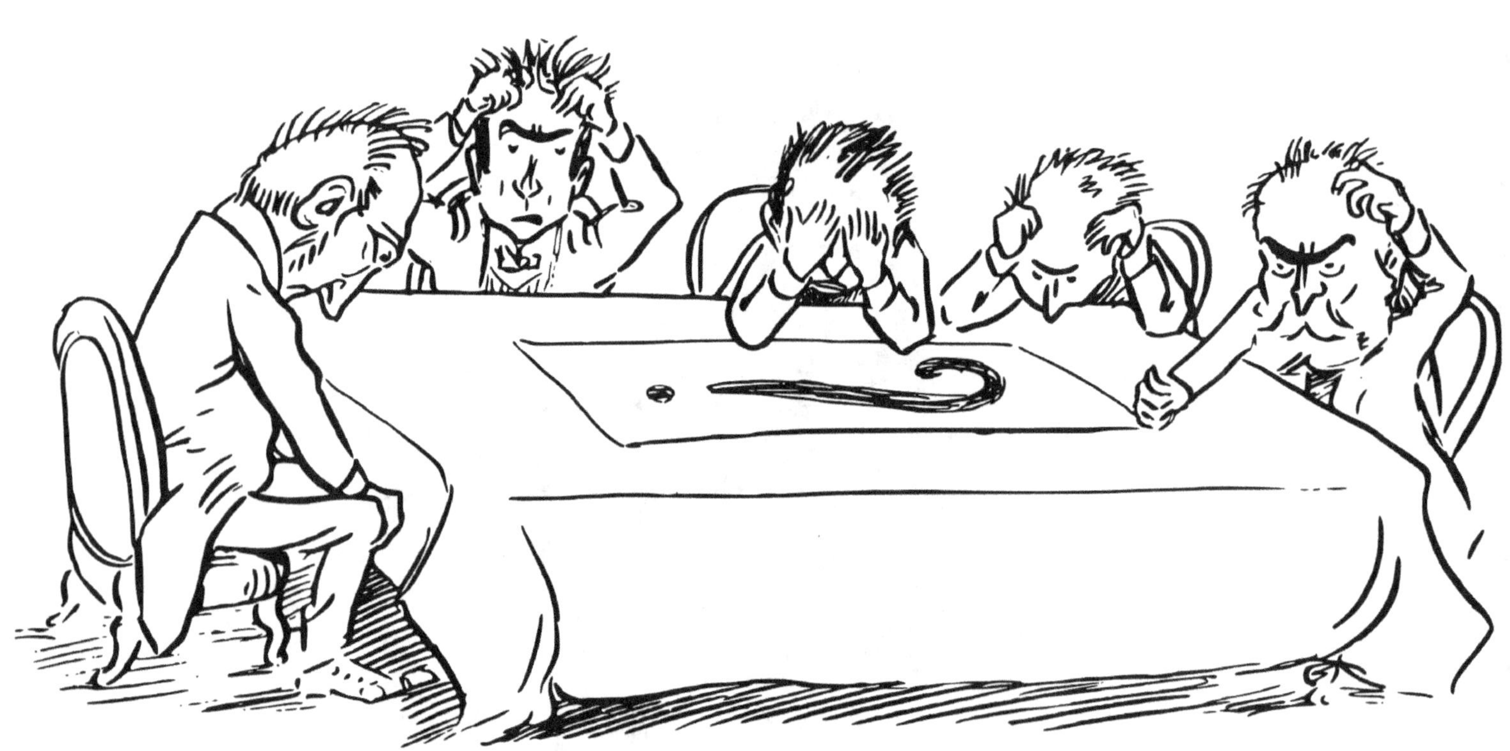

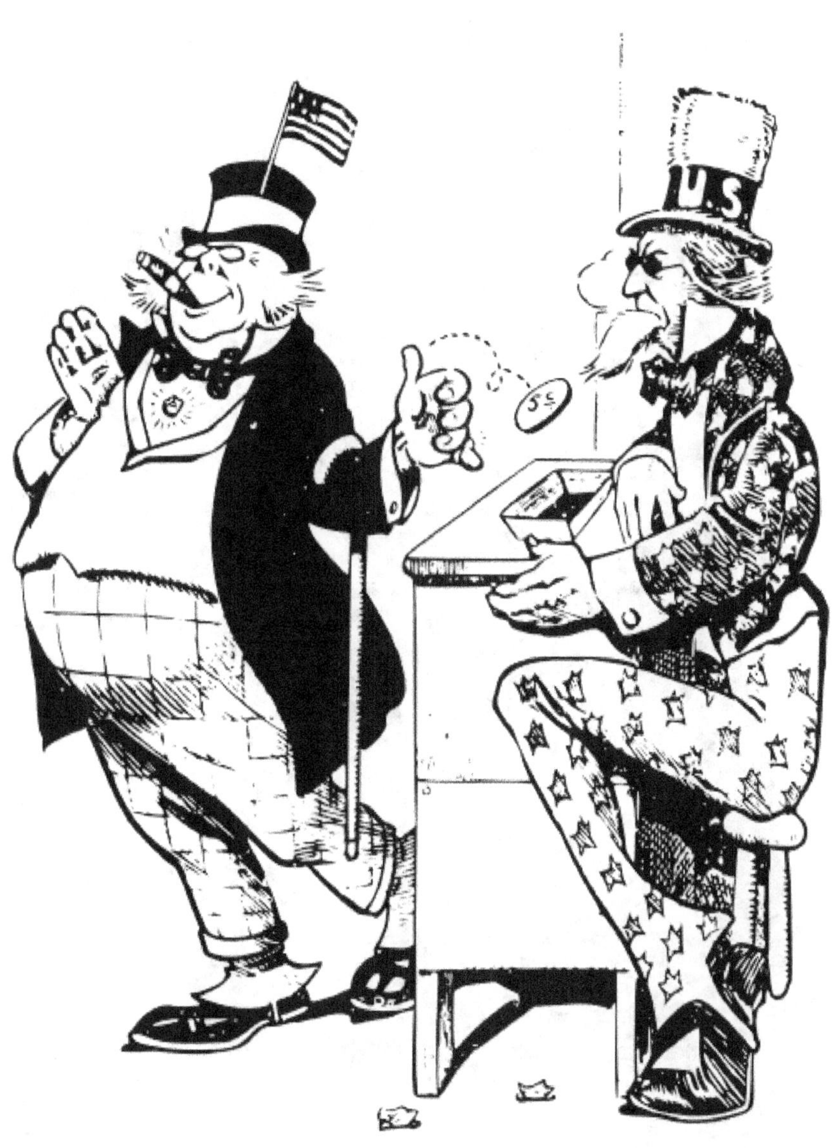
U.S.
5¢

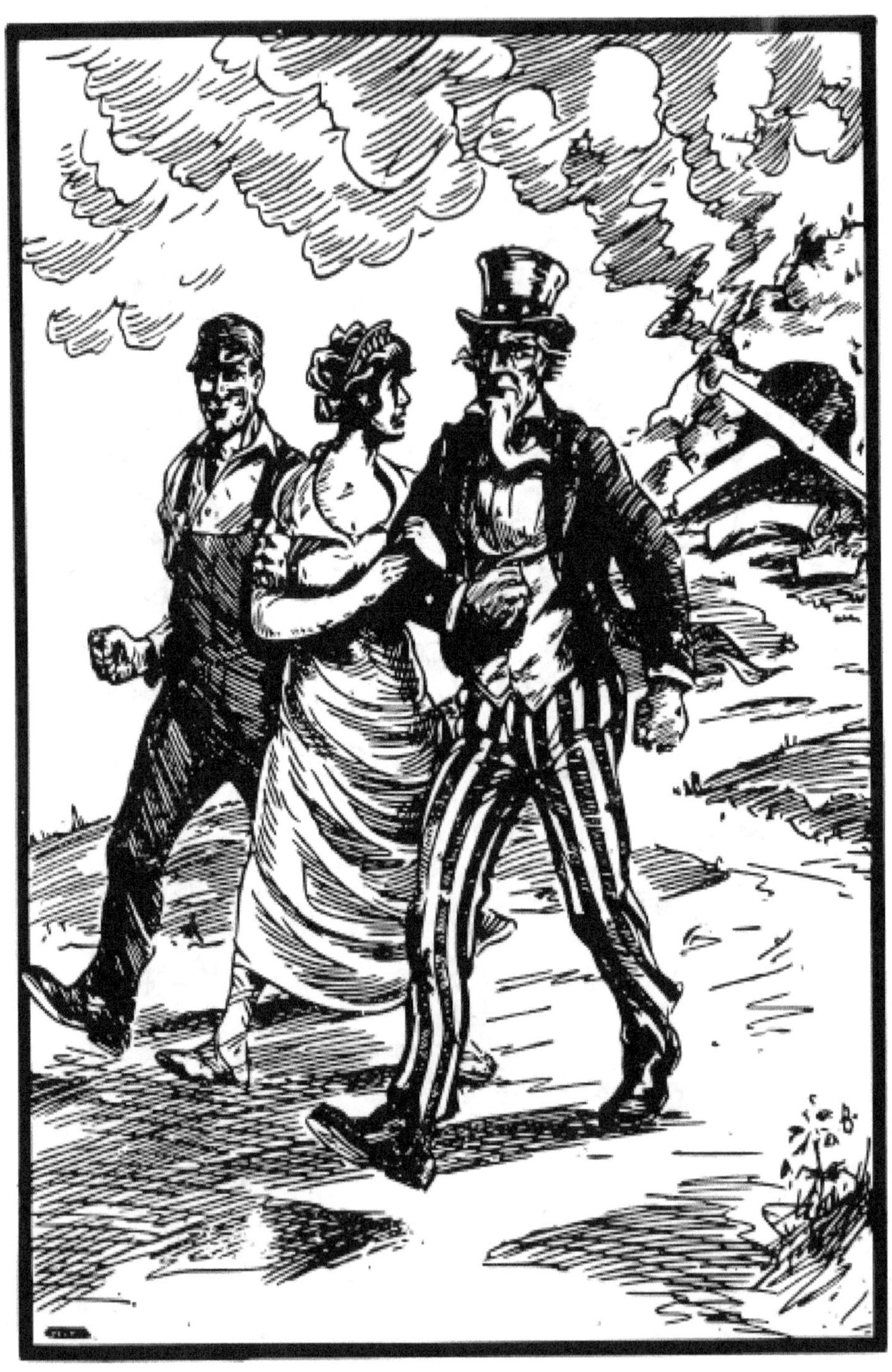

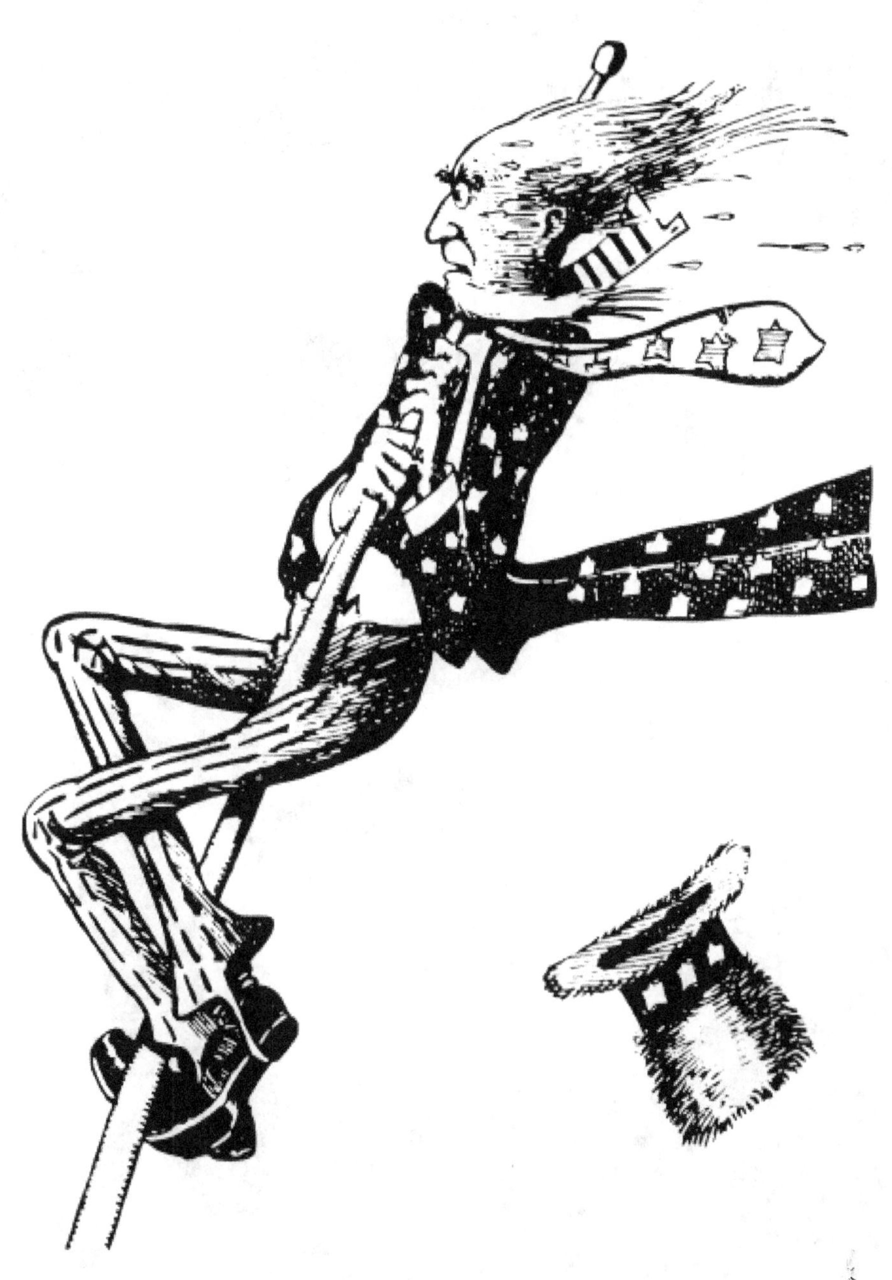

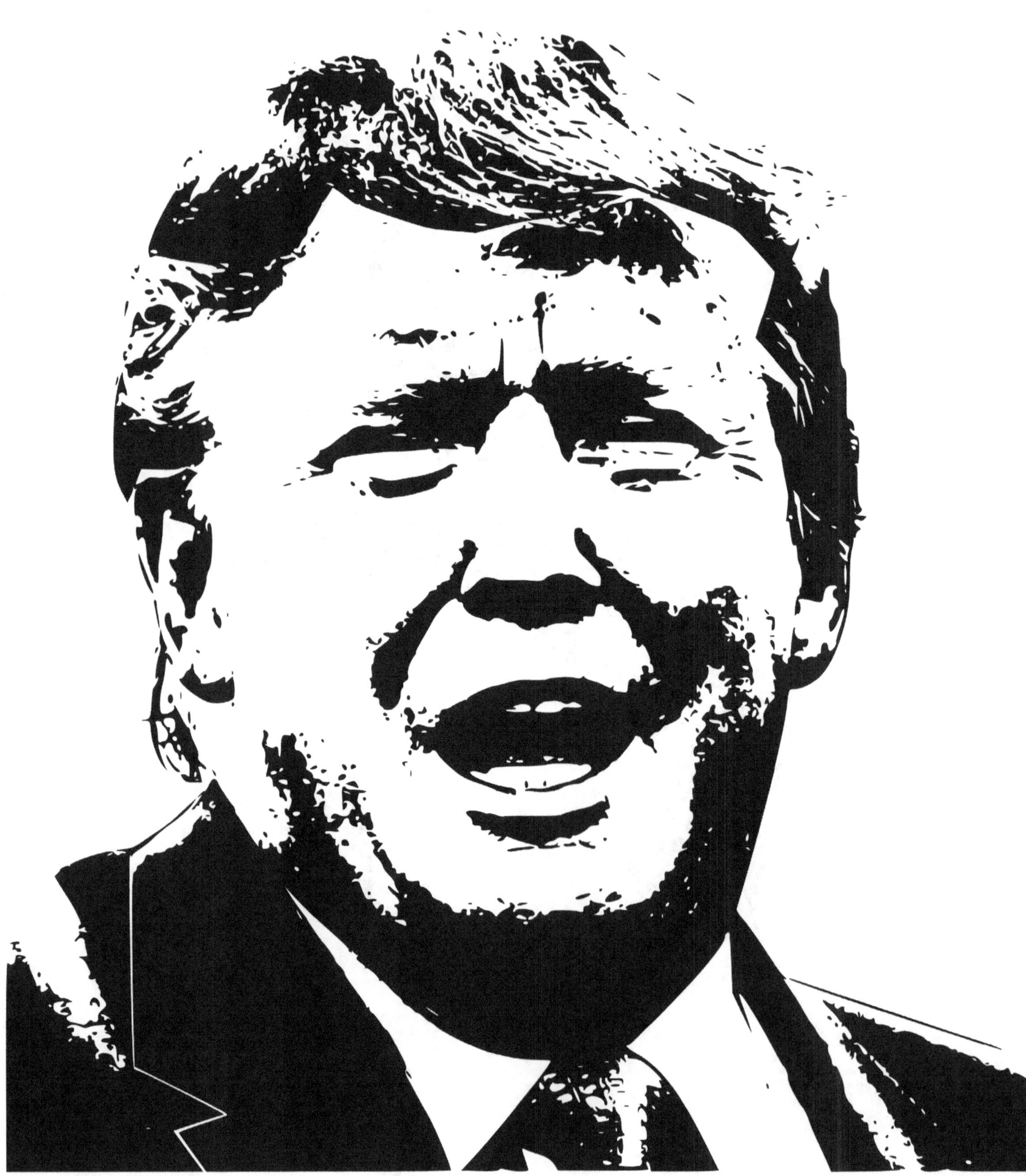

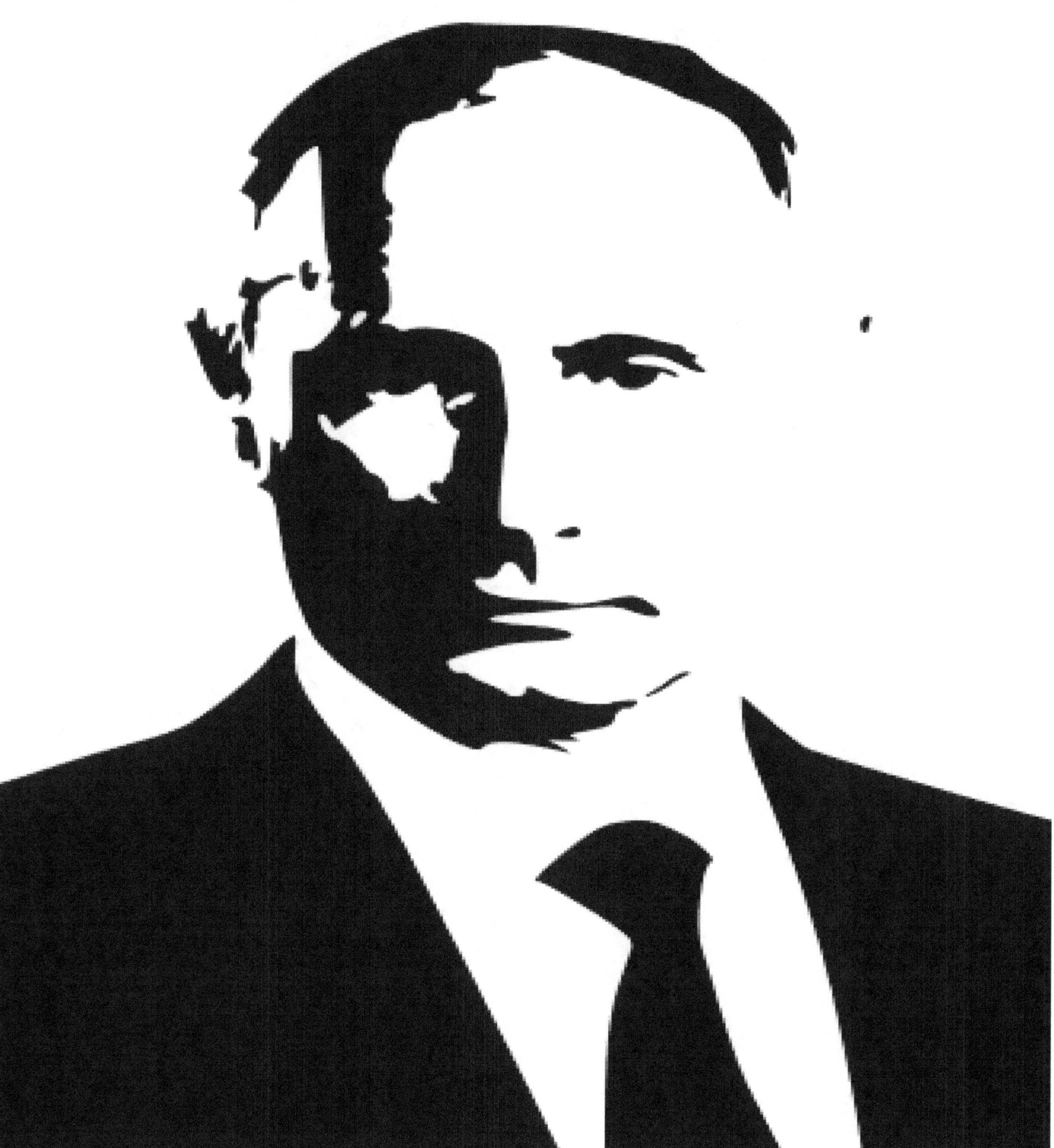

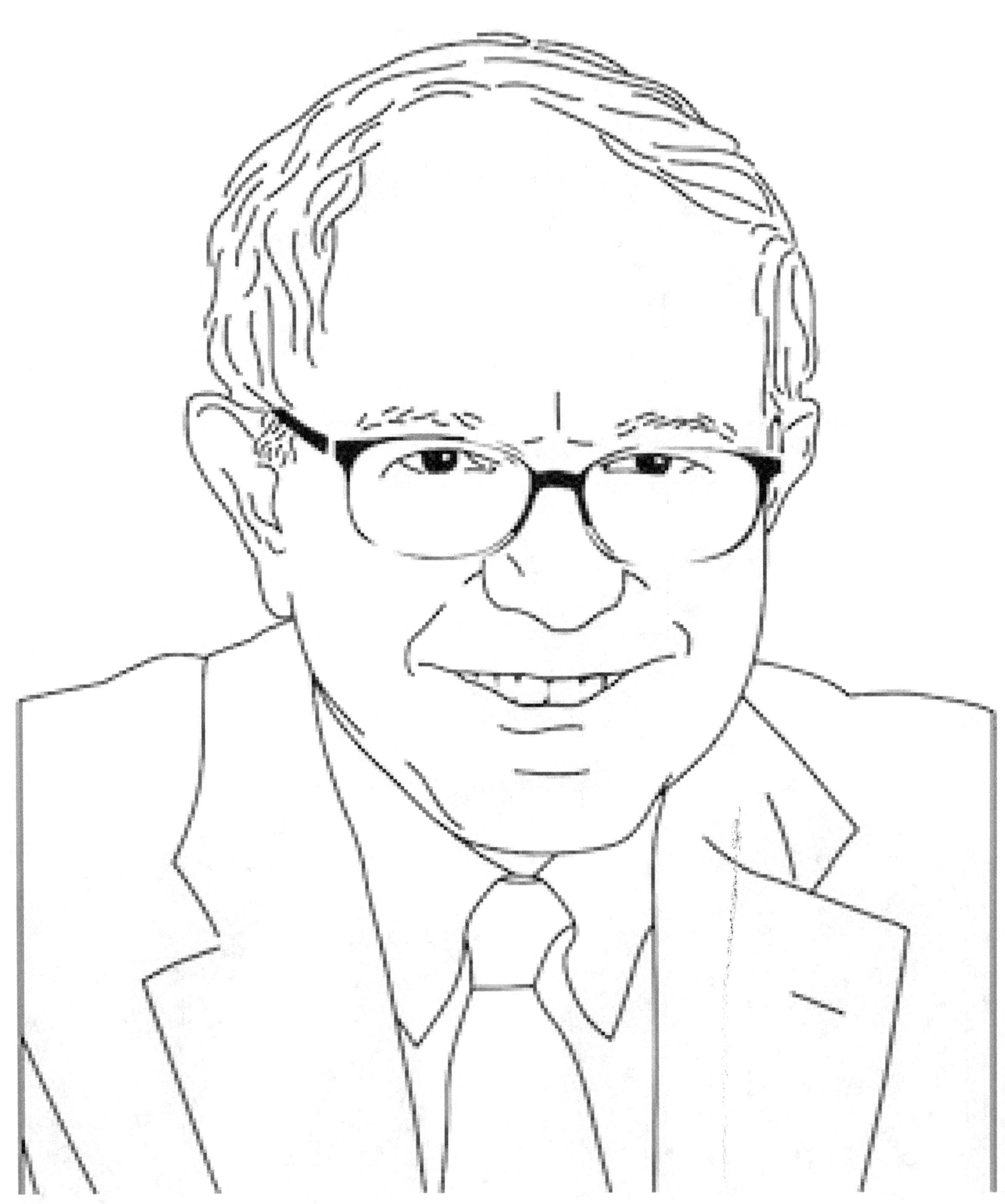

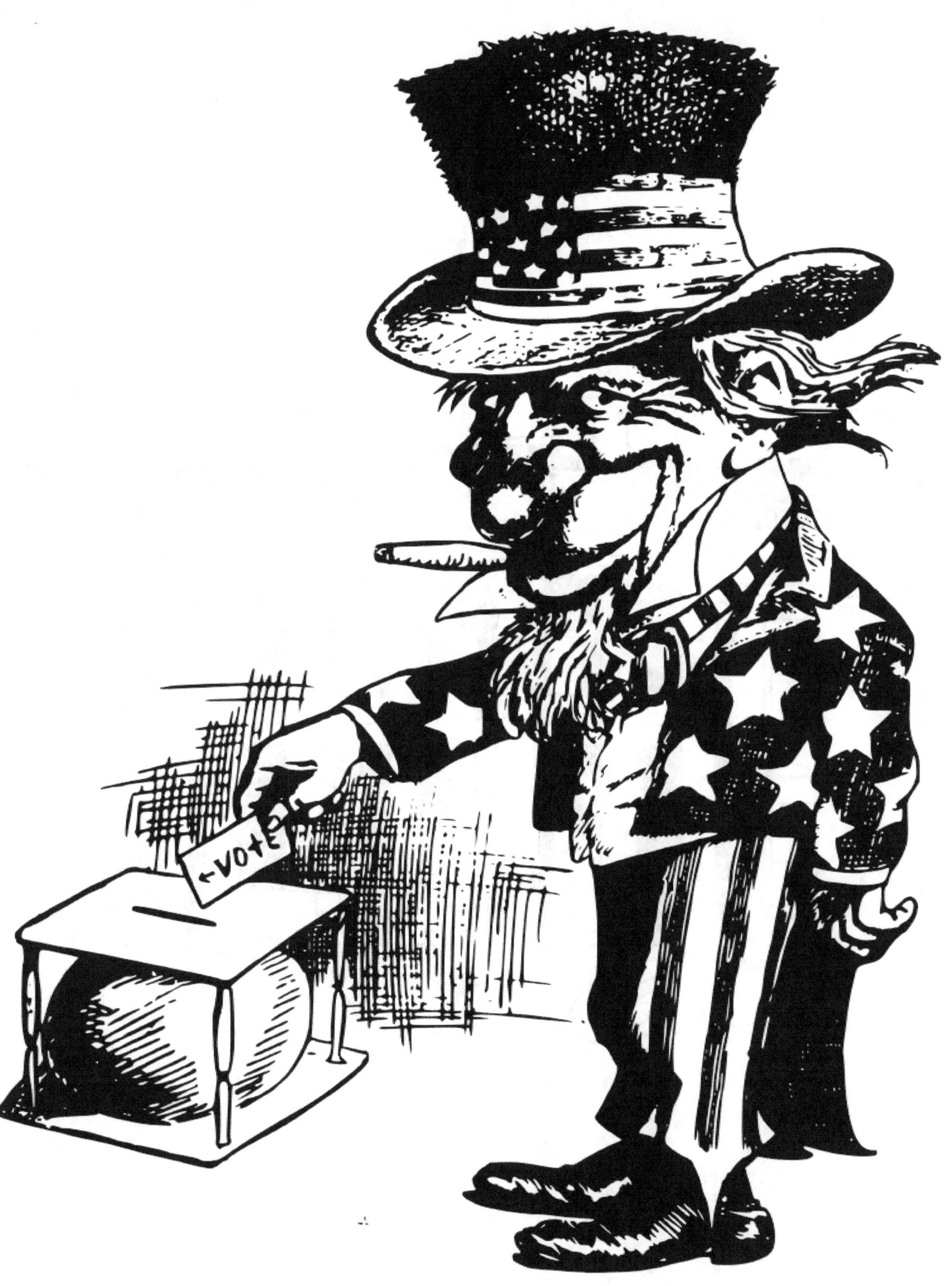

VOTE

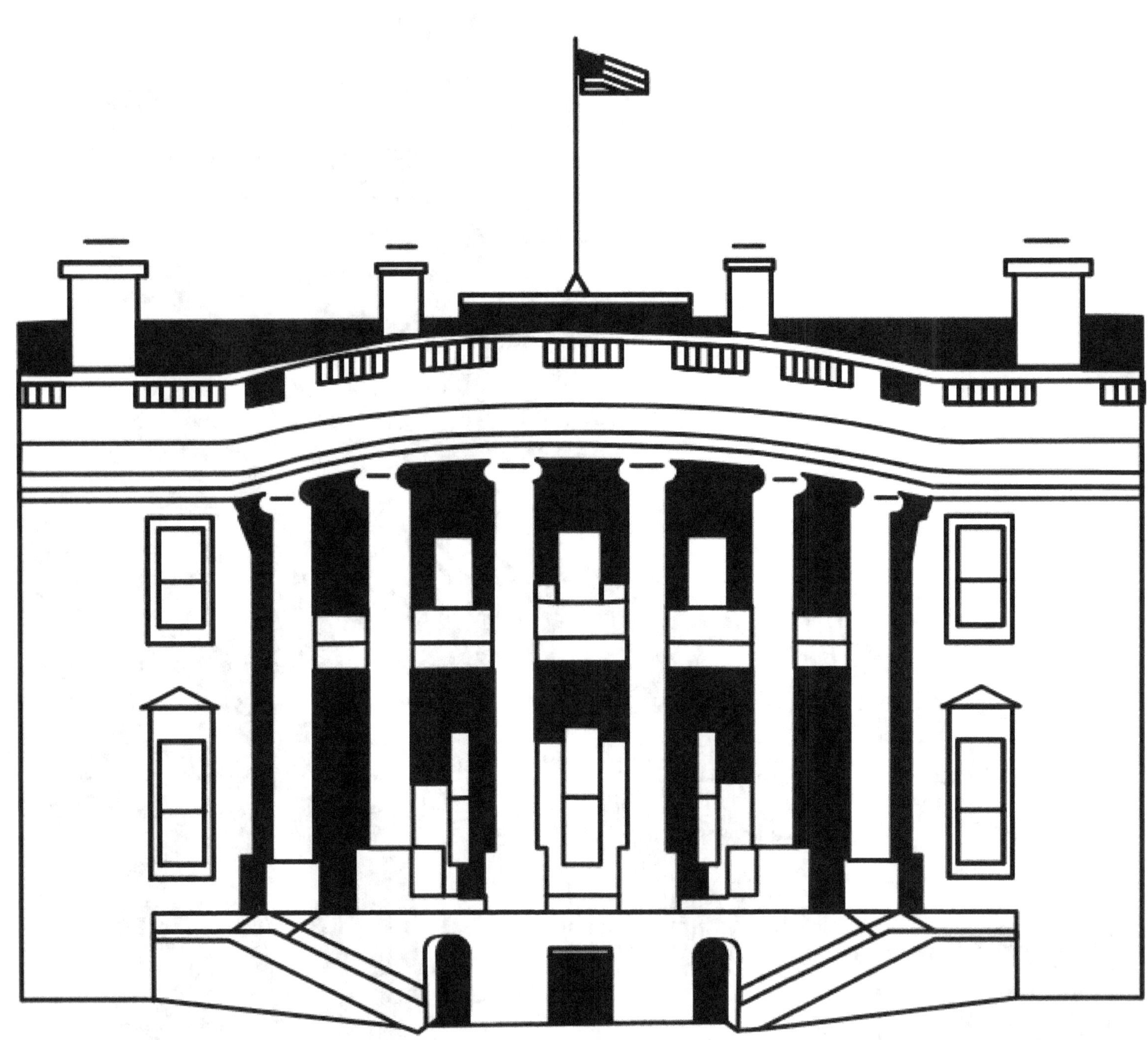

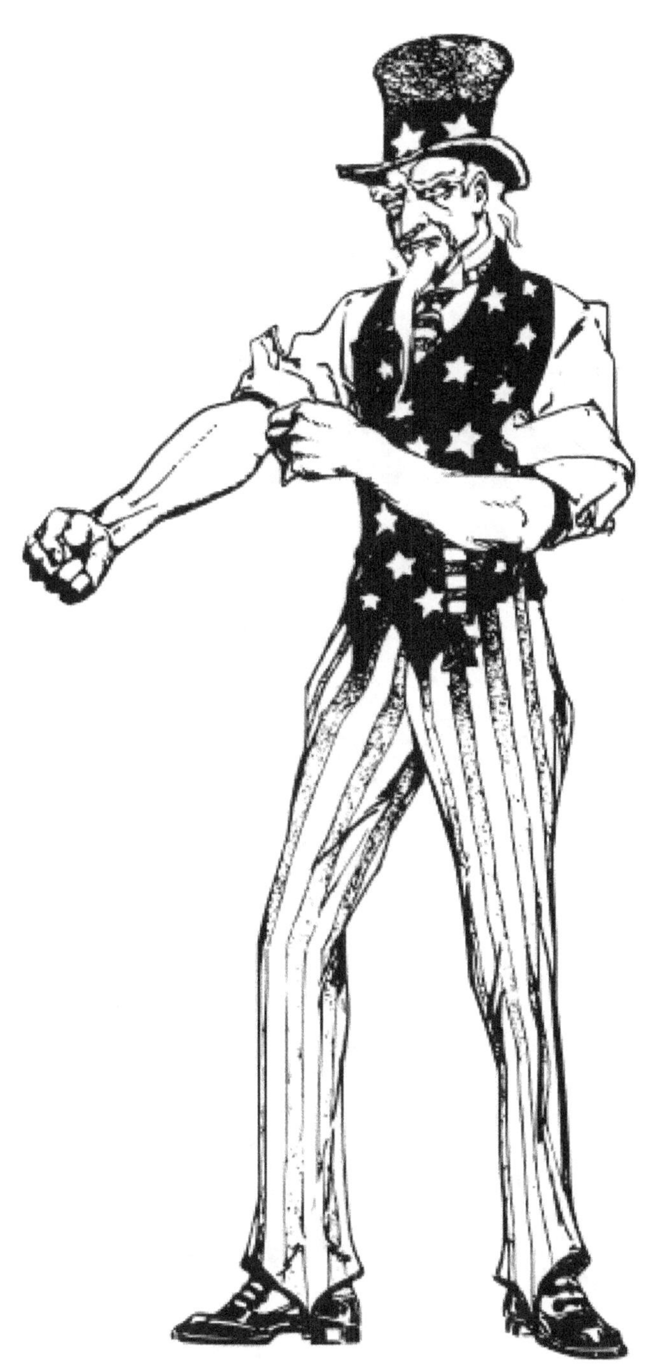